21st Century Skills Library

LIFE SKILLS BIOGRAPHIES

BILL AND MELINDA GATES

Dana Meachen Rau

Cherry Lake Publishing
Ann Arbor, Michigan

Published in the United States of America by Cherry Lake Publishing
Ann Arbor, MI
www.cherrylakepublishing.com

Content Adviser: Josh McHugh, Contributing Editor, *Wired*, San Francisco, California

Photo Credits: Cover and pages 1, 24, 25, 35, and 41, © Reuters/Corbis; page 5, © Warren Toda/epa/Corbis; page 6, © Dan Lamont/Corbis; pages 7, 10, and 11, © Bettmann/Corbis; page 13, © Doug Wilson/Corbis; page 16, © David Jay Zimmerman/Corbis; page 17, © Roger Ressmeyer/Corbis; page 21, © Najlah Feanny/Corbis; page 22, © Owen Franken/Corbis; page 28, © Justin Lane/epa/Corbis; page 30, © Gates Foundation/Corbis; pages 32 and 40, © Naashon Zalk/Corbis; page 36, © Lou Dematteis/Handout/epa/Corbis; page 38, © Brian Wallace/Corbis Sygma; page 42, © Corbis/Corbis

Library of Congress Cataloging-in-Publication Data
Rau, Dana Meachen, 1971–
   Bill and Melinda Gates / by Dana Meachen Rau.
      p. cm. — (Life skills biographies)
   ISBN-13: 978-1-60279-068-1
   ISBN-10: 1-60279-068-X
   1. Gates, Bill, 1955—Juvenile literature. 2. Businesspeople—United States—Biography—Juvenile literature. 3. Computer software industry—United States—History—Juvenile literature. 4. Microsoft Corporation—History—Juvenile literature. 5. Gates, Melinda, 1964- 6. Bill & Melinda Gates Foundation—History—Juvenile literature. I. Title. II. Series.
   HD9696.63.U62G3755 2008
   338.7'610053092273—dc22
   [B]   2007006956

*Cherry Lake Publishing would like to acknowledge the work of
The Partnership for 21st Century Skills.
Please visit www.21stcenturyskills.org for more information.*

CONTENTS

INTRODUCTION

Once you are hugely successful and enormously wealthy, what comes next? What would you do with billions of dollars? Bill and Melinda Gates are two of the richest people in the world. They are taking the energy they once poured into their jobs at Microsoft—the software company Bill founded more than 30 years ago that transformed how people use computers—and turning it toward philanthropy. Through their foundation, they are finding ways to spread their wealth so that others can have an equal chance of success in life.

❧

CHAPTER ONE

THE BEGINNINGS OF WEALTH

Bill and Melinda Gates are using their time and money to give back to the worldwide community.

The Microsoft empire began with the dreams of a competitive and curious boy. William Henry Gates III, known as Bill, was born in Seattle, Washington, on October 28, 1955. His father, William Henry Gates II, was a lawyer, and his mother, Mary Gates, was a teacher. Bill had an older sister and a younger sister—Kristiane and Libby.

The United Way helps support food banks and other organizations that help people in communities throughout the United States.

Bill's family was wealthy. Their money had in large part come from Bill's great-grandfather, who founded the First National Bank in Seattle in 1911. Bill's parents could provide many things for their children, but the family did not keep all of the wealth to themselves. They gave their money and time to several charities. Mary was a leader in United Way, a charitable organization that brings communities together to help people in need, and William was also active in charitable groups. Mary often talked with the family about her work with the organization and about the best way to give to others. In a 2006 speech, Bill remembered, "We talked about how much of our allowances we should be giving to the church, to the Salvation Army. And, you know, it really got us thinking about the impact of giving."

Bill was an intensely curious child, and he loved to read. He read an entire set of encyclopedias from A to Z before he was nine. He also enjoyed just sitting and thinking. In 1962, when he was seven years old, the World's Fair was held in Seattle. It attracted millions of people who came to see the

Bill always had a competitive spirit and loved to play games. In fact, his family called him Trey. *Trey* is a card-playing term for "three," and because he was the third William H. Gates, the name suited him. His family spent a lot of time playing games together, like Monopoly or Risk, and he liked to win. During their summer vacations to the shores of the Hood Canal, an inlet of Puget Sound, his family set up elaborate Olympic-type competitions of games and sports, such as waterskiing.

The famous Space Needle building in Seattle was built for the 1962 World's Fair.

many exhibits devoted to science, entertainment, art, and business as well as ones about what life might be like in the future. Among the high-tech exhibits on computer technology, Bill saw large mainframe computers on display and learned about the role computers might play in the future.

Bill was very bright, and school was easy for him. He didn't have to work very hard to get good grades, so he was often bored. He was much smaller than most kids his age, and his classmates often teased him. He didn't seem to fit in. He was almost too smart to relate to the other kids. Plus he knew he was smarter than many of them, and he let them know it.

Bill had trouble at home, too, often arguing with his parents. They decided to send their son to Lakeside School, a private boarding school in the area that could provide more challenging courses and perhaps some focus. Bill was 12 and did not want to go. "In those days, Lakeside was an all-boys school where you wore a jacket and tie, called your teachers 'master,' and went to chapel every morning. For a while, I even thought about failing the entrance exam," Bill said in a 2005 speech at the school. But in 1967, he started school at Lakeside.

CHAPTER TWO

FINDING HIS WAY

Bill Gates grew up and went to school in Seattle, Washingon.

At Lakeside, Bill wound up being happy, though not necessarily with the schoolwork. Math and science were his best classes, and he discovered interests in drama and sports. While he still found most of his classes boring, he was pushed by his teachers to work up to his potential. And he was still cocky, calling some of his peers stupid. He would talk about how he was going to become a millionaire. But Bill did make some friends. He found a group of boys who were as smart as he was and shared a common hobby with him—computers. Computers soon became an obsession.

The earliest computers were much larger
than the computers we use today.

Computers were gaining popularity in the early 1960s. At that time, they were large machines that often filled an entire room and that only large companies or government organizations could afford. Other people could connect to those computers with a phone connection and a teletypewriter, a printing device used to send and receive signals via phone lines. Lakeside had such a machine hooked up to a big mainframe computer at another location through a phone line. Bill spent hours in McAlister Hall on Lakeside's campus, working on the machine. He even snuck over there at night when he should have been in bed.

At the time, some "people were actually afraid of what the computer might do to them," Bill later recalled. Teachers were also nervous about using the device because every moment they spent on it cost the school money, and they didn't want to waste that money making mistakes experimenting with this relatively new machine. "I emerged as the person who was confident enough to play with it," Bill said, "and I ended up getting picked to actually teach the computer classes at my high school."

International Business Machines Corporation (better known as IBM) was an early leader in the field of information technology and computer development.

Bill Gates turned his childhood hobby of creating software for computers into an extremely successful business.

The physical parts of the computer are the hardware. But to run, a computer needs software, the programs that tell the computer what to do. And creating programs is what Bill and his friends spent time doing. "You had to type up your program off-line and create this paper tape," he explained in a speech at Lakeside many years later, "and then you would dial up the computer and get on, and get the paper in there, and while you were programming, everybody would crowd around, shouting: 'Hey, you made a typing mistake. Hey, you messed this up! Hey, you're taking too much time.'"

He and his friends, including an upperclassman named Paul Allen, formed the Lakeside Programmers Group. They wrote programs for the computer, including a game of tic-tac-toe. But the group was spending so much time on the computer that they had to find a way to help pay for their time. So they started a business writing software.

Bill Gates and Paul Allen started working together when they were both students at Lakeside School.

And soon, they had several clients. The school hired them to create software to work out class schedules. The Computer Center Corporation hired them to fix bugs in the system and make sure its security features worked. When Bill was only 15, he and Paul created Traf-O-Data, a program to measure the way traffic moved, to help the city study traffic patterns and solve traffic problems. For this program, the two boys supposedly made $20,000.

Bill Gates entered Harvard University in 1973.

Bill was ready to leave school and start his own software business with Paul. But his parents insisted he stay in school. In the fall of 1973, Bill headed to Harvard University, in Cambridge, Massachusetts, to study law like his father had. Bill approached school with his usual competitive spirit, taking classes, spending time in the computer center, and hardly sleeping. As he recalled in a 2006 speech, "I was taking way more than a normal number of classes, and having a great time doing it."

However, he soon read a magazine story that would change his life. He and Allen, who worked in a town near Cambridge, read the article featured on the cover of the January 1975 issue of *Popular Electronics* with great excitement. It introduced the Altair 8800 microcomputer, a box with lights and switches that could be programmed. And Gates and Allen both knew it had the potential to change the world.

Immediately, they wrote to the company, MITS, in Albuquerque, New Mexico, and offered to write the software for the computer. The company agreed, and the two young men worked day and night writing the software in Harvard's computer center.

Gates and Allen were dreamers. They knew that computers would not always be the large mainframes they were used to. They imagined "a computer on every desk and in every home." And with the Altair 8800 on the market, they wanted to act fast. They did not want to be left behind. In a 2006 speech, Gates remembered that "even then we could see that the idea that an individual would sit down, organize their information, organize documents, look at how their business was running, communicate with other people, we saw that this could be an incredible tool."

Life & Career Skills

Bill Gates's decisions in life have often been surrounded by a sense of optimism. He started Microsoft just as computers were becoming smaller and, therefore, more accessible to everyone. "The one thing I did know is that I saw the computer could be important," he said during a 2006 speech, "and I loved to read a lot, I was very curious, and so I just kept pursuing that curiosity with a lot of energy and a lot of optimism that neat things might happen." And they did.

Starting a new business can be risky. Luckily, Bill Gates's family was wealthy, so he did not have to worry if the business didn't work out. But he wanted to make his own money. One trait all new business owners share is a sense of self-direction. Gates knew what he wanted, and he was willing to work hard to get it. And since he was passionate about computers, he was able to work in a field he truly enjoyed.

The software for the Altair worked. So Gates dropped out of Harvard during his junior year, and at only 19 years old, he and Allen moved to Albuquerque, where they started the software company that they had dreamed about in high school. They called it Microsoft.

Gates and Allen started Microsoft in Albuquerque, New Mexico.

CHAPTER THREE

THE GROWTH OF MICROSOFT

```
TO SKETCH1
  ST
  SETXY ( ( 128 - PADDLE 0 ) * 135 / 128
  ) ( ( 128 - PADDLE 1 ) * 110 / 128 )
END

TO WAIT :TIME
  IF :TIME = 0 STOP
  MAKE "TIME :TIME - 1
  WAIT :TIME ; >>>>>>>> 50 = 1 SECOND
END

"NUM1 IS 16
"NUM2 IS 53
"ANSWER IS 69
"REPLY IS 71
"COM IS
"VY IS 0
"VX IS 0
"COMMAND IS
"COUNTER IS [ ]
"INPUT IS 71
?
```

A computer screen shows a series of programming commands

Gates and Allen wrote the software for the Altair in the computer language BASIC, which stands for Beginner's All-purpose Symbolic Instruction Code. The MS-BASIC program (the MS stands for Microsoft) was a part of the package sold with every Altair. Gates and Allen wanted to retain ownership of the program, and Gates's instinctive business sense kicked in. He fought to keep the right to sell the software to other microcomputer makers as well. He believed that microcomputers (later to be called personal computers, or PCs) were the future for the computer industry.

Gates moved Microsoft to Bellevue, Washington, in 1979.

Microsoft had grown as a company, added employees, and moved to Bellevue, Washington, which is just east of Seattle, in 1979. In 1980, IBM, another computer company looking to grow in the personal computer market, asked Microsoft to design the whole operating system for their computers. The operating system is the program that makes the computer perform all of its basic operations and run its programs. Microsoft would also write the software.

For this new agreement with IBM, Gates and Allen adapted an existing operating system and created MS-DOS (Microsoft Disk Operating System). As with the Altair, they sold the operating system to IBM but kept the right to sell it to other manufacturers. And they did. With tremendous sales, Microsoft grew throughout the early 1980s at a rapid pace. Allen resigned as executive vice president in 1983 due to illness but remained on the company's board of directors. Gates continued to forge ahead. In 1985, Microsoft released another operating system called Windows.

Microsoft now had 1,000 employees, and in 1986, Gates moved the company's offices to Redmond, Washington. The new headquarters was like a college campus with beautiful buildings and lawns. Gates surrounded himself with super-intelligent people. He wanted his company to be a place where these superior minds could collaborate on great ideas as they developed new products.

Life & Career Skills

Bill Gates has never been a typical business leader. His youthful appearance and creative nature make him different. He does not dress in a suit and tie. He sees his work as fun. Microsoft employees (called Microsofties) work in a casual atmosphere where they are urged to be creative.

But Gates works incredibly hard and sets high standards for himself—and he expects his employees to do the same. This has created a team of very talented and driven people. He expects his employees to ask the right questions and have the right answers.

By the late 1980s, Microsoft was the largest software company in the world and Bill Gates was a billionaire.

The late 1980s were an important time for Gates. Microsoft became the largest software company in the world. Most personal computers sold came with a package of Windows software. Gates had become a billionaire at age 31. He also met Melinda French.

Born August 15, 1964, Melinda had grown up with her parents, Raymond and Elaine, and two brothers and one sister in Dallas, Texas. At St. Monica Elementary School, one of Melinda's teachers noticed her mathematical talents. "She put me in an accelerated group—a bunch of boys and me," Melinda said at the Texas Conference for Women 2005. "I worked harder than I had ever worked before, and it was thrilling."

Melinda was passionate about computers. When she was in high school at Ursuline Academy, not all schools had access to computers. But a math

Like Bill Gates, Melinda French was passionate about computers.

The Apple II got Melinda French hooked on computers.

teacher at Melinda's high school was able to get Apple II computers for her class, and Melinda was hooked. She graduated from Ursuline as the valedictorian of her class in 1982. She decided to go to Duke University in Durham, North Carolina, and majored in both computer science and economics. After she graduated in 1986, she stayed on at Duke to earn her master's degree in business in 1987.

Right out of business school, this intelligent, independent businesswoman was hired by Microsoft. With the company, Melinda managed multimedia products, such as the encyclopedia called Encarta. Gates was always tough on people he met, just like when he was young. He only liked to surround himself with people he felt were smart enough, and French was one of those people.

"After a number of years of dating, we decided we were good partners," French said in a 2004 interview. Gates, 38, and French, 29, got married in Hawaii on New Year's Day 1994, on a cliff with a view of the ocean. Two years later, the couple had their first child, Jennifer. At that time, Melinda had risen to the level of general manager of Information Products, but she decided to leave Microsoft to be home with Jennifer. Bill and Melinda have two other children: Rory was born in 1999, and Phoebe in 2002. Melinda has tried to keep their family life out of the media. "I want to live as private a life as I can because of our children," she has said. She often declines interviews.

In 1997, the family moved into a $54 million mansion in Medina, Washington, a secluded place with mountain views. The mansion itself is very high-tech, many of its features run by computers. Music is piped into numerous rooms. The house has an expansive library and game room. There are guest quarters, a trampoline room, and a 30-car garage.

Bill Gates published *Business @ the Speed of Thought* in 1999. In this book, he details how business and technology are interconnected and how to use this relationship to enhance workplace productivity.

The Gates family lives in a mansion in Medina, Washington.

Back at work, Bill turned his attention to the Internet. By the early 1990s, more and more people were surfing the Web and using computers as tools to communicate with each other. Bill, who had usually been the first to foresee people's computer needs, was not the first to create tools for using the Internet. Another company, Netscape, had already created a browser, a program people use to surf the Web.

Bill's competitive nature kicked in. He created a browser, Microsoft Explorer, and packaged it with all of the other Microsoft Windows software. Soon he had taken over the market.

Not everyone felt Bill was a great businessman. When he launched Windows, he was accused of stealing an idea from one of his top competitors, Apple Computers. Gates's system used a style of windows and icons similar to those that Apple had been using for many years. And because Microsoft programs came with almost every personal computer,

Steve Jobs (above) is one of the founders of Apple Inc., one of Microsoft's competitors.

After a three year trial, the Federal Trade Commission and Microsoft reached a settlement in the monopoly court case on November 2, 2001.

people started to wonder if that was fair. No other software companies would ever be able to crack into the market. Customers were never given a chance to choose what software they wanted.

In 1998, the Federal Trade Commission, the part of the United States government in charge of making sure businesses are fair, took a closer look at Microsoft. They believed the company was an illegal monopoly—that it unfairly locked competitors out of the software market—and the government filed a lawsuit against the company. There was talk that

Microsoft might have to break into two companies. Bill was devastated. After several years of hearings and trials, it ended up that Microsoft would stay intact.

Bill had always liked to be in charge. But with the stress of the government concerns about his company, he was beginning to feel the pressure of running Microsoft. And now he had a family. In 2000, he stepped down as chief executive officer (CEO). Steve Ballmer, a close friend of Bill's from college who had been with him as Microsoft grew, became CEO. Bill would become chief software architect, and in this role, he would be able to get his hands back into programming.

Microsoft continued to grow. It released new and improved versions of Windows as the needs of its customers changed. It created gaming systems such as Xbox, released in 2001. And the dream that started with two young men imagining a computer in every home is close to true—and most of those computers are using software he has created.

When two teams compete, an official such as a referee or umpire makes sure they are playing fair. That means each has an equal chance to win.

But what if one team was so good that the other team wasn't even allowed on the field? The government accused Microsoft of being a monopoly, claiming that other software companies never had a chance to "play" in the game.

What do you think? Is being the best still winning if you didn't actually play another team?

CHAPTER FOUR

WHAT GIVING CAN DO

Over the years, Bill Gates had received many requests for money from people in need. After all, he's been the richest man in the world since the mid-1990s. People thought he might have some money to spare. Though he had given away some of his money, he hadn't planned to start philanthropy work until he retired. Making money and giving it away at the same time seemed odd to him. "During the day you make money . . . and then you go home and you start giving it away, and maybe you'd get confused about which thing you were doing," he said at a 2006 award presentation.

Because Bill was worth billions, people didn't think he was giving away enough of his money. In 1994, his father wanted to help address some of those requests for aid. Bill agreed. "I believe that with great wealth comes great responsibility," he said at a 2006 news conference, "a responsibility to

Bill Gates (left), Melinda Gates (middle) and Warren Buffet (right) held a press conference in 2006 to announce that Buffett was donating $30 billion of his money to the Bill and Melinda Gates Foundation.

give back to society, a responsibility to see that those resources are put to work in the best possible way to help those most in need."

So he and his father set up an organization, which was initially called the William H. Gates Foundation, and Bill Sr. headed it from the recreation room in his basement. A few years later, Bill and Melinda created a foundation that focused on providing Internet access to libraries in low-income areas and giving students more learning opportunities. In 2000, the two foundations merged under the name the Bill and Melinda Gates Foundation.

Bill and Melinda were trying to decide the best way to give away their money. They looked at the impact their wealth could have in their local area in Seattle, then looked at the larger needs of the United States and finally at the needs of the world. They decided to focus their charitable work on the issues of global health and education.

"One day, Melinda and I read an article about the millions of children who were dying every year in poor countries from diseases that we had long ago eliminated in this country," Bill said in a 2006 speech. "One disease . . . was killing literally half

Learning & Innovation Skills

What would you do if you were the richest person in the world? Would you spend all the money on yourself? Would you keep it so that you could pass it on to your children? Would you try to solve problems in the world? If so, which ones?

Rotavirus is the most common cause of life-threatening diarrhea in children. For most people, being infected with this virus is not a serious illness. But infected infants and young children are especially at risk for dehydration. If those infected are unable to replenish the fluids lost during the course of the disease, they might need to be hospitalized for treatment. In developed countries, few children die from infection because they have access to modern health care and hospitals. Sadly, this is not always the case in poorer countries.

a million kids a year. I thought: That's got to be a typo. If a single disease was killing that many kids, we would have heard about it—it'd be front-page news. But it wasn't."

Melinda Gates speaks to some children during a trip to India.

In addition, they learned that thousands of children and adults were dying every day of other preventable and treatable diseases, such as malaria, which is a blood infection caused by a parasite, and tuberculosis, a bacterial infection that most often affects the lungs. Bill and Melinda found the number of deaths staggering.

"World health is something where, when you first realize the situation, it's pretty stark and even a bit depressing—just the magnitude of the inequity," Bill said when named one of *Time* magazine's Persons of the Year. It was unfair, the couple agreed, that the lives of children didn't seem to be valued equally around the world. If a child in a rich country died, it was seen as tragic. But the millions of children dying in Africa from treatable diseases was hardly news. They decided to run the Bill and Melinda Gates Foundation based on the core value that "all lives, no matter where they are being led, have equal value."

Bill and Melinda don't just read reports and articles about what is happening in the world. They take what they call learning tours. They travel thousands of miles a year to visit regions in need of assistance. They visit hospitals, where situations are often dire and medicine and equipment needed

Learning & Innovation Skills

Complex problems, such as inequality, can seem unapproachable. But thinking carefully and critically about their causes can help in finding solutions.

While the horrible situations in the world can be overwhelming, Bill and Melinda enjoy the challenge of trying to solve some of the world's problems. As Bill said in 2006, "One thing I hope more people learn is that giving and giving with a lot of thinking . . . and thinking through these problems can be immensely fun."

to keep people alive are in short supply. They also go to homes and community centers in small villages, where they can talk with people about the challenges they are faced with every day.

Bill and Melinda know that just giving people money, or buying food or medicine for them, won't necessarily solve their problems. So they are looking for long-term solutions, such as ways to prevent or cure diseases that afflict millions worldwide. And no matter how much money the couple has, they know they can't do it themselves. That is why they rely on

Bill and Melinda Gates visit a health center in Mozambique.
The health center received money from the Bill and Melinda
Gates Foundation to fund malaria research projects.

the expertise of others and look for ideas that can change the world. "We are funders and shapers—we rely on others to act and implement" is one of the foundation's guiding principles.

The foundation tries to excite governments to work with them and encourage businesses to get onboard to help solve the problems. The foundation gives grants to groups working for solutions. For example, they gave out 500 million dollars in Grand Challenges Grants. These grants were given to the best scientists in their fields to help solve the problems of global health, including innovations like medicines that can be stored without refrigeration. Another group, the Global Alliance for Vaccines and Immunizations, has been given millions of dollars to get vaccines to children in poor countries so that deaths from treatable diseases won't be an everyday occurrence.

Fighting malaria is one of the foundation's top priorities. In many poor, hot countries where mosquitoes carry the disease, children are often victims. This is especially true throughout Africa, where 2,000 children die every day from malaria. The Bill and Melinda Gates Foundation has given generously to the Malaria Vaccine Initiative, which is working to create vaccines to stop the spread of malaria. The focus of this work is not only in developing a vaccine, but in getting scientists, the vaccine manufacturers, the government, and health workers together to distribute the vaccine to all who need it.

Besides working in the area of global health, the foundation also strives to help reduce poverty and increase technology in poorer countries. In northern Bangladesh, where rivers often flood the land and there is

Bill Gates had a great knowledge of technology that he wanted to share. One thing he hoped for was that people all over the world could have access to computers.

In 1997, he had donated a computer to a community center in Soweto, a very poor area of South Africa. When he arrived, he saw a huge extension cord running more than 200 yards (183 meters) from a generator to the computer in the community center, which didn't have its own electricity. Bill realized that the moment he left, they would probably use the power for more important things. His computer was pretty much useless to them.

Bill saw that, in many places, for technology to be useful, it had to be used in a different way. In some places, using technology to make discoveries, develop new medicines, and deliver them to the people who need them are more important than having access to a computer.

no electricity or phone service, villagers crowd the docks to get onto boats that hold computers, books, and teachers. The Bill and Melinda Gates Foundation has helped fund these boats, which visit villages along the rivers. People who would normally be cut off from information can surf the Internet. Adults also learn new farming and business methods, and children go to school.

The foundation also seeks to improve the lives of people in the United States. Many grants are given to organizations that work to increase the number of U.S. students who graduate or to improve the type and quality of education in U.S. high schools. Imagine a high school where students get to build a pool table or even a submarine. That is what Bill imagines in newly designed high schools. "The U.S. high schools, although they were great for their time, are now having big problems," he said in a 2006 speech in South Africa. "And they're not really giving most [students] a good education in the things they need to know for the jobs that exist."

*Bill Gates visits one of the libraries in South Dakota that received funds
from the Bill and Melinda Gates foundation to purchase computers.*

He and Melinda have been dismayed by how many kids drop out of
school before graduation, and how unprepared graduates are for jobs in
the modern workplace. At a 2006 Seattle conference on education, he said,
"We need to change the system. We need to ensure that all our kids are
ready for school, ready for college, and ready for work." A redesigned high
school might mean fewer students take fewer courses but focus on projects
in which they can test what they've learned to see if it works.

Bill Gates accepts the James C. Morgan Global Humanitarian Award for his charitable efforts around the world.

They also give money to provide free Internet access in libraries throughout the United States. In their home state, their donations to the Washington Families Fund and the Sound Families Initiative have made life more hopeful for homeless families there. The money helps people get training for new jobs and pays for child care. It also helps to build affordable homes so that people have safe, stable environments to raise their families. The goal is for these families to become self-sufficient again.

All of the Bill and Melinda Gates Foundation's contributions are based on one main idea: everyone should be considered equal and, therefore, be given equal opportunities for success in the world.

Bill's and Melinda's business sense, focus, and optimism have worked well for them while running the foundation. "A lot of skills I learned at Microsoft are absolutely skills I rely on and use at the foundation," Melinda said in a 2004 interview. Just as he is with Microsoft's earnings, Bill is careful about how his money is going to be spent and makes sure none of it is wasted.

In 2005, *Time* magazine named Bill and Melinda Gates (along with U2 lead singer Bono) its Persons of the Year for the work they have done in poorer countries. Melinda is one of *Forbes* magazine's 100 Most Powerful Women. Bill received the James C. Morgan Global Humanitarian Award in 2006. The Bill and Melinda Gates Foundation is the largest charitable foundation in the world, with an endowment of more than $30 billion, and is a leading force of change in the world today.

21st Century Content

In developing countries, two-thirds of deaths in children under age five stem from health problems that are preventable or treatable with existing tools. Malaria kills 2,000 African children every day. HIV/AIDS kills more than 3 million people a year—99 percent of them in developing countries. Tuberculosis kills someone every 18 seconds. Acute diarrheal illness kills up to 3 million children a year. Acute lower respiratory infections kill up to 2 million children a year.

CHAPTER FIVE

MAKING THE WORLD
A SMALLER PLACE

Bill Gates's innovative ideas have had a profound impact on the way people around the world live their lives.

"I have decided that two years from today, starting July 2008, I will reorder my personal priorities," Bill Gates announced at a press conference on June 15, 2006. Instead of channeling all his energies into Microsoft, he will be working full-time for the Bill and Melinda Gates Foundation.

Bill will not completely leave Microsoft behind. He will be handing over the company to people who he knows will continue its success. And he will not retire.

He will still be Microsoft's chairman and advise the company on new products in development. But he wants to focus his energies on the foundation, working alongside his wife.

Melinda and Bill have made a good team running the foundation. "I think this is very much a collaborative effort," said Melinda in a 2004 interview. "We come at it from slightly different angles, but that's why it's a natural for us to do it together." Together they have already helped many, and they have great plans for helping more.

Bill and Melinda's influence will continue to have an impact on the world. In 2007, Microsoft released its newest operating system, called Vista. And of course, Microsofties are always developing new ways to use technology. "Twenty-three years from now, I am optimistic enough to think that computers will be so powerful they'll almost disappear," Bill said at a 2006 conference. "As you walk into your house, you'll simply be able to speak out loud and say what TV shows [you] might . . . be interested in, and it will hear your voice, recognize that, see who you are, and bring the right thing up on the screen. Most of the things you read, magazines, newspapers, you won't need those."

Bill will often bring stacks of books with him when he goes on vacation. He also has what he calls Think Weeks. He'll take time off of work to read books, articles, and papers about topics related to work or his philanthropy. "I definitely think of myself as a lifelong learner," Bill has said.

Bill sees a future where connections will all be wireless. Satellites will help people communicate over long distances, so that remote places, such as parts of Asia and Africa, will be more connected to the technology other parts of the world have enjoyed. But it will not just bring those people information. "These advances are going to allow us to make the world smaller, allow us to see the suffering, but also the ability to treat it," Bill said in a 2006 speech. "Advances in technologies can also help us deliver these things, so we don't just invent them, we make sure they get out there."

Bill and Melinda Gates continue to fight hunger, disease, and poverty around the world.

With the work at the foundation, the couple also sees a bright future. "I will say that 23 years from now we'll have vaccines for the diseases that have created such a problem and were not addressed up until now," said Bill in

Bill Gates speaks out about his foundation's efforts to slow the spread of HIV/AIDS in India at a news conference in New Delhi in 2002.

2006. "I'd certainly say we'll have a vaccine for malaria, tuberculosis, [and] given that time frame even AIDS, which is the toughest, I think it's very likely."

And what's best is that the foundation continues to grow. It will move into a new headquarters in the middle of Seattle, with an ambitious building program that began in 2007. The world has seen what Bill and Melinda have done and that it has made a difference. Their example has encouraged other wealthy people to give money. In 2006, Warren Buffett,

Melinda Gates watches as Queen Elizabeth II presents her husband with his honorary knighthood in recognition of their many charitable contributions.

a fellow billionaire, began donating a large amount of his fortune to the Bill and Melinda Gates Foundation.

"All of us are very blessed and we enjoy what the world has given us, and it also has given us the opportunity to do the important work of reducing inequities," Bill said upon accepting the James C. Morgan Global Humanitarian Award in 2006. "I can't think of anything that's worth more of our time and effort."

Bill and Melinda have many responsibilities in their lives. Bill is still responsible for Microsoft and running the company well. They are responsible for their family and raising their children. Melinda has talked about these responsibilities in many interviews and speeches. "We definitely step back once a month and say, 'Did we as a couple spend time on the right issues, be it the foundation, Microsoft, our children?'" Melinda says. "And if it ever gets where it feels like it's not the right balance, then we reshuffle."

But they feel they have a responsibility to the world, too. "The premise of this foundation is one life on this planet is no more valuable than the next," Melinda says. And she wants to teach this to her own children. "Bill and I wanted to begin teaching our children, at an early age, about hands-on philanthropy and the duty they have to help others."

Melinda remembers her mother-in-law, Mary Gates, giving a short speech at an event before Bill and Melinda's wedding. Mary read from a letter she had written to the couple, which said, "From those to whom much is given, much is expected." Mary and Bill Sr. had given much of their time and money. "She wanted to make sure that her son and I did the same," says Melinda, "and much more."

Timeline

1955   William H. Gates III (Bill) is born on October 28.

1964   Melinda French is born on August 15.

1967   Bill goes to Lakeside School.

1973   Bill goes to Harvard University.

1976   On November 26, the trade name Microsoft is registered with the Office of the
         Secretary of the State of New Mexico.

1979   Microsoft moves to Bellevue, Washington.

1980   Bill and Paul create the MS-DOS operating system for IBM.

1985   Microsoft introduces its first version of the Windows operating system.

1986   Melinda graduates from Duke University with a bachelor's degree in computer
         science and economics; Microsoft moves to Redmond, Washington.

1987   Melinda graduates from Duke University's Fuqua School of Business with a
         master's in business; she is hired by Microsoft; Bill and Melinda meet.

1994   Bill and Melinda marry on January 1; Bill creates the William H. Gates
         Foundation to give to organizations that focus on global health and community
         needs.

1996   Melinda leaves Microsoft to take care of their daughter, Jennifer.

1997   Bill and Melinda start the Gates Library Foundation, providing computers and
         Internet access to public libraries.

1998   The U.S. government files a lawsuit against Microsoft.

1999   The Gates Library Foundation becomes the Gates Learning Foundation, focusing on education; son Rory is born.

2000   The William H. Gates Foundation and the Gates Learning Foundation merge to become the Bill and Melinda Gates Foundation.

2001   A settlement is reached in the U.S. Justice Department lawsuit against Microsoft.

2002   Daughter Phoebe is born.

2005   Bill and Melinda Gates (along with Bono) are named *Time* magazine's Persons of the Year.

2006   Bill announces he will step down from Microsoft by 2008 to devote himself full-time to the foundation; the foundation reorganizes its giving into three areas: Global Development, Global Health, and United States.

2007   Bill receives honorary degree from Harvard University.

GLOSSARY

browser (BROU-zur) a computer program that enables you to surf the Internet

charitable (CHA-ruh-tuh-buhl) giving money or help to people in need

collaborate (kuh-LAB-uh-rate) to work together by sharing ideas and having discussions

endowment (en-DOW-muhnt) a large amount of money meant to continue the operation of a company or foundation

foundation (foun-DAY-shuhn) an organization that gives money to help worthwhile causes

grants (GRANTS) gifts of money to use for a certain purpose

hardware (HARD-wair) the physical parts of a computer

mainframe (MAYN-fraym) a large, powerful computer that can take up an entire room

microcomputer (MYE-kroh-kuhm-PYOO-tur) a small computer for an individual to use; now known as a personal computer

monopoly (muh-NOP-uh-lee) complete control over a service or the supply of a product

multimedia (MUHL-tye-MEE-dee-uh) using different methods of sharing information, such as text, pictures, video, and maps

operating system (OP-uh-ray-ting SISS-tuhm) the program that makes the computer perform all of its basic operations and run its programs

optimism (OP-tuh-mizm) a sense of hopefulness and happiness

philanthropy (fuh-LAN-thruh-pee) active effort to help others by giving time or money

self-direction (SELF duh-REK-shuhn) one's own guidance or supervision

software (SAWFT-wair) the programs you use on a computer that tell it what to do

FOR MORE INFORMATION

Books

Heller, Robert. *Business Masterminds: Bill Gates*. London: Dorling Kindersley, 2000.

Lee, Lauren. *Trailblazers of the Modern World: Bill Gates*.
Milwaukee, WI: World Almanac Library, 2002.

Lesinski, Jeanne M. *Just the Facts Biographies: Bill Gates*.
Minneapolis: Lerner Publications Company, 2005.

Peters, Craig. *Bill Gates: Software Genius of Microsoft*.
Berkeley Heights, NJ: Enslow Publishers, 2003.

Woog, Adam. *Bill Gates*. San Diego, CA: KidHaven Press, 2002.

Web Sites

The Bill and Melinda Gates Foundation
www.gatesfoundation.org
For the latest information about the foundation, its founding, and its mission

Centers for Disease Control and Prevention
www.cdc.gov/
Features details on diseases, where they are found and who
they affect, and their causes and treatments

Microsoft
www.microsoft.com
Includes information about the company and its software

INDEX

ABOUT THE AUTHOR

Dana Meachen Rau is the author of more than 200 books for children. She has written a variety of nonfiction titles on many subjects, including books on history and science, as well as biographies, toys, and crafts. When she is not writing in her home office in Burlington, Connecticut (using Windows software, of course!), she is playing with her children, creating art, or keeping busy in her community.